Science Close-Up
GEMSTONES

Written by Gina Ingoglia
Illustrated by Paul Lopez

A GOLDEN BOOK • NEW YORK
Western Publishing Company, Inc., Racine,Wisconsin 53404

What Are Gemstones?

Many kinds of rocks lie deep inside the earth. People dig them out and put them to many uses. We build with huge blocks of rock like granite and marble. We pave roads with tiny rocks called gravel. We use different forms of rock to make other things—even glass!

Rocks are made up of minerals. These are naturally occurring materials that have their own individual makeup and properties. Sometimes unusual changes take place underground and rare rocks are formed. These rare and beautiful rocks are gemstones.

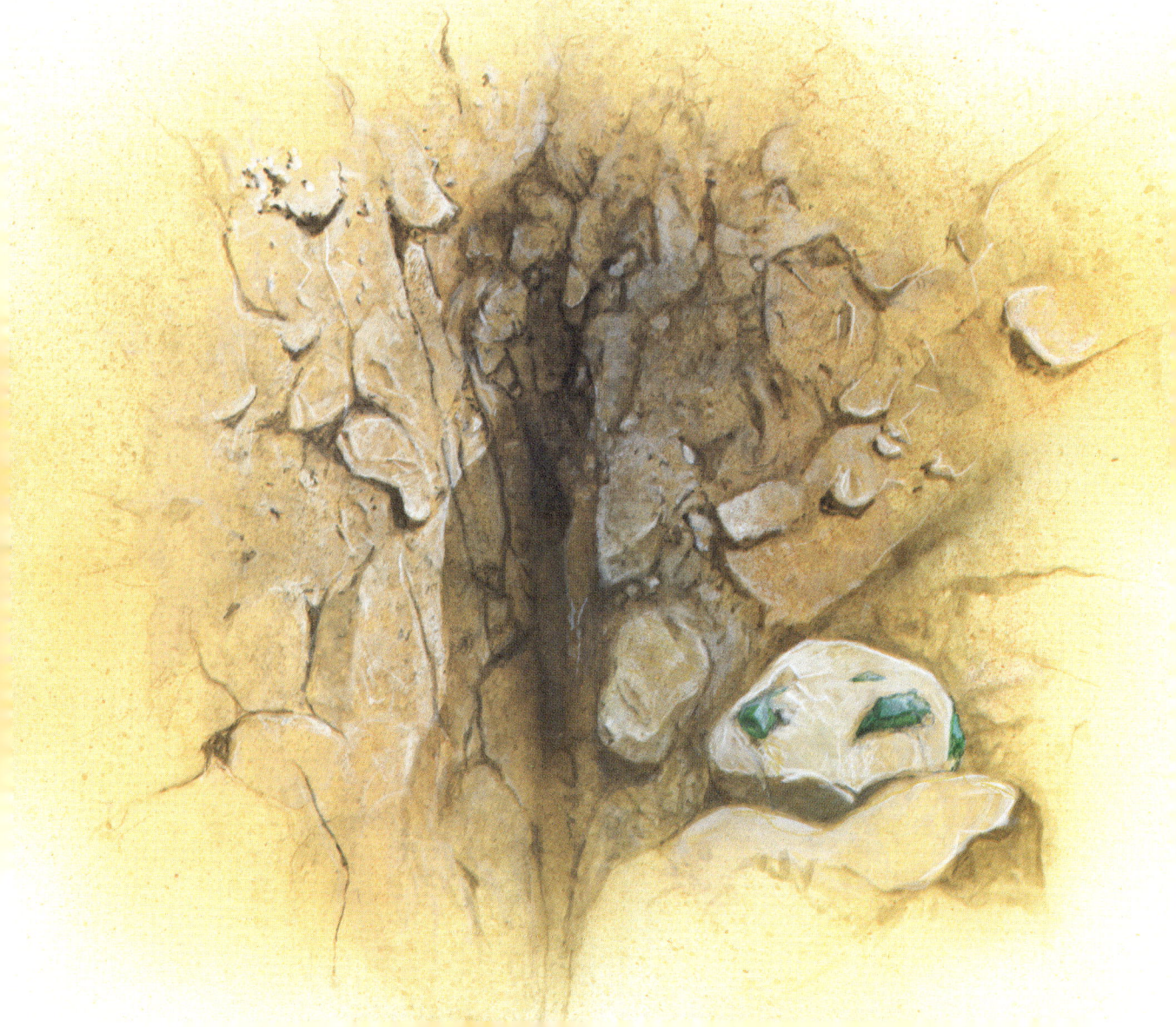

sapphire

ruby

blood ruby

Not Quite the Same!

People file their fingernails with gritty strips of cardboard called *emery boards*. The rough coating is made up of tiny bits of gray ground-up rock called *corundum*. But a chunk of blue corundum is a valuable **sapphire** gemstone, and red corundum stones are **rubies**! The rarest gemstone in the world is a dark red ruby. It is called a **blood ruby**.

rose quartz

tiger eye

bloodstone

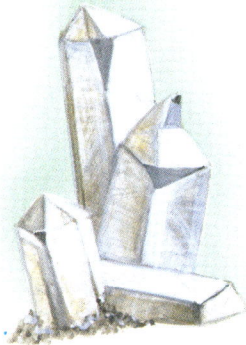

milky quartz

amethysts

Glass is made from a whitish mineral called *quartz*. Pink-colored quartz is a gemstone called **rose quartz**. Striped pieces of quartz are **tiger eye** gems. Some quartz is called **bloodstone** because it contains red speckles. **Milky quartz** is cloudy because of tiny fractures or "bubbles" in the quartz. Purple quartz stones are **amethysts**. They are the most valuable form of quartz.

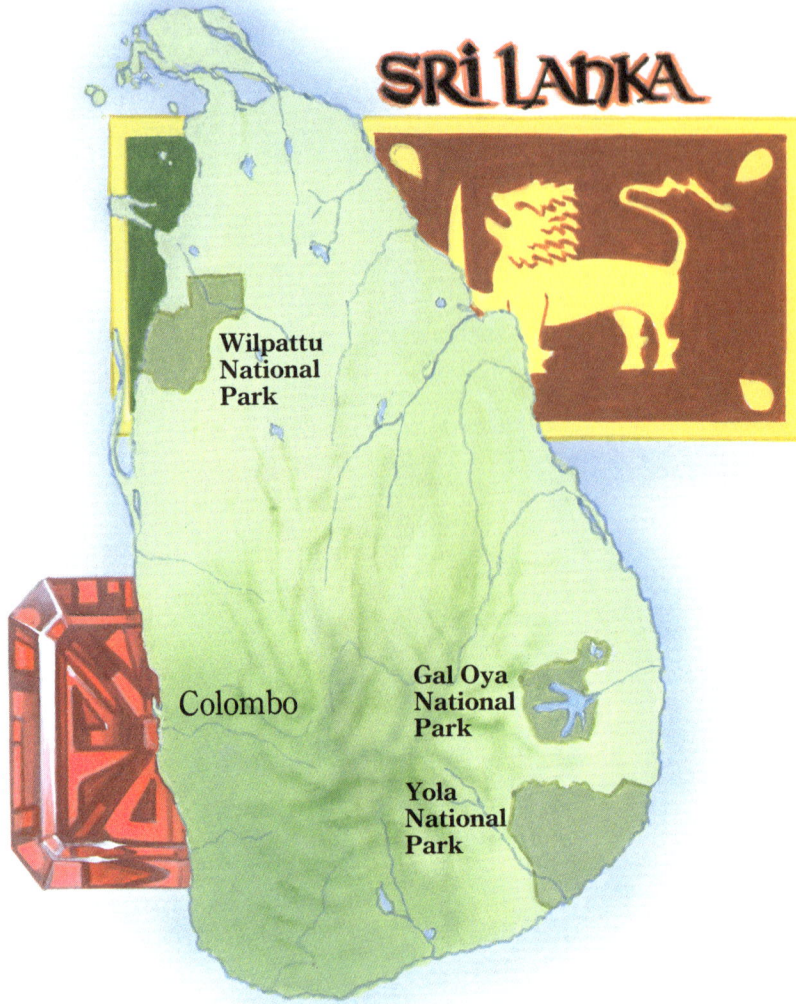

SRI LANKA

Wilpattu
National
Park

Colombo

Gal Oya
National
Park

Yola
National
Park

"Gem Island"

Sri Lanka, a small island nation in the Indian Ocean, has been nicknamed Gem Island because so many kinds of gemstones are found there.

The gems are inside rocks high on the mountains. During storms called typhoons, heavy rains wash rocks and mud down the sides of the mountains. Gem hunters or miners poke long poles into this muddy soil until they hit underground gravel that may contain gems. Then they dig pits, sometimes as deep as fifty feet, and climb into them to hand up scoops of muddy stones. The mud is put in large flat baskets. Standing in waist-deep water, other miners strain away the mud. If they are lucky, they find a valuable gemstone or two.

What Is a Lapidary?

Some gemstones are clear and sparkle in the light. These are called *transparent gemstones*. When they are first found, they aren't as pretty as the finished stone. To become real "gems," these stones must be cut and polished.

A person who cuts, shapes, and polishes gems is called a *lapidary*. Before cutting a stone, the lapidary studies it from all angles. This could take days or even weeks! If the stone is not cut just right, it might crumble. The cut stone is then held against a fast-spinning wheel and polished. Polishing creates great heat and is more dangerous than cutting. Too much heat can shatter a valuable gem, turning it into a worthless pile of dust!

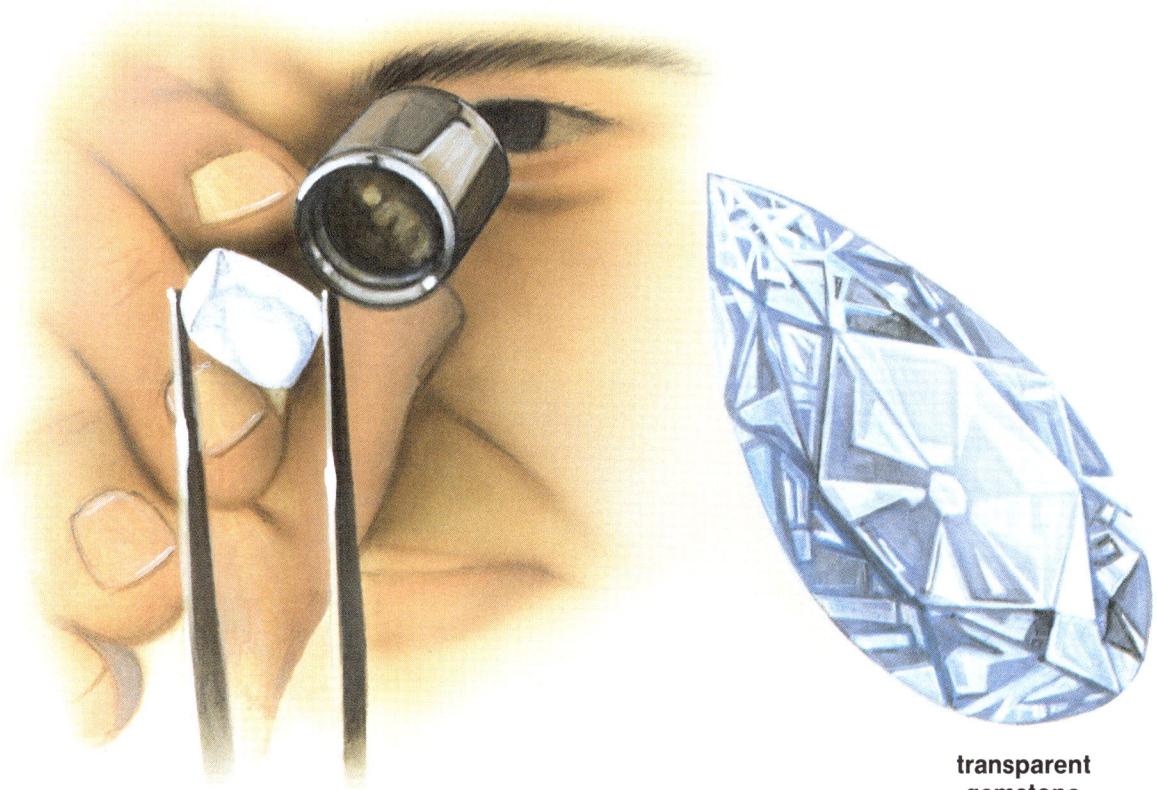

transparent gemstone

diamond in natural state

blue diamond

pink diamond

yellow diamond

black diamond

A Lucky Find

Many **diamond** gemstones look like clear, sparkling ice. But there are also black, yellow, pink, and blue diamonds.

Diamond mining began in India about 2,500 years ago. In 1725 more diamonds were found in Brazil. In those early days, diamonds were rare and expensive gems. Only very rich people owned them.

In 1866 a fifteen-year-old farm boy named Erasmus Jacobs found a diamond in a riverbank in South Africa. His lucky find was the beginning of that country's famous diamond-mining industry. Because so many diamonds are found there, more people can afford to buy them today.

Harder Than Anything

Nothing on earth is harder than a diamond! A diamond can be cut only by another diamond. It can be sharpened sharper than a razor.

Most diamonds aren't perfect enough to become gems, but they have other important uses. These are industrial diamonds. They are used in surgical instruments and in tools for making electric light bulbs. Because diamonds can withstand extreme pressure, some are sliced thin and used as tiny windows through which pictures are taken by space probes.

cutting a diamond with a diamond

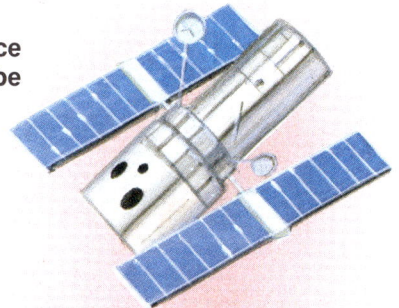

space probe

diamond and razor

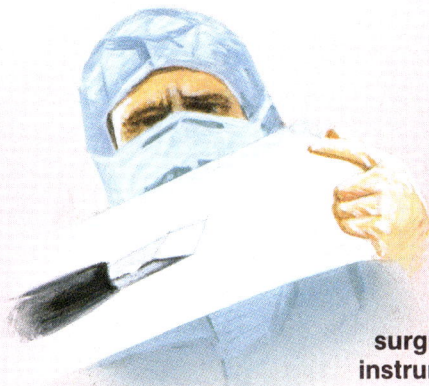

electric light bulb tool

surgical instrument

Two Secret Trips

In 1905 the world's biggest diamond was found in South Africa. A mine manager named Frederick Wells saw the huge diamond stuck in a chunk of rock, and he pried it out with his pocketknife. Gem weights are measured in *carats*. This diamond, as big as an orange, weighed 3,106 carats! That's about 1⅓ pounds!

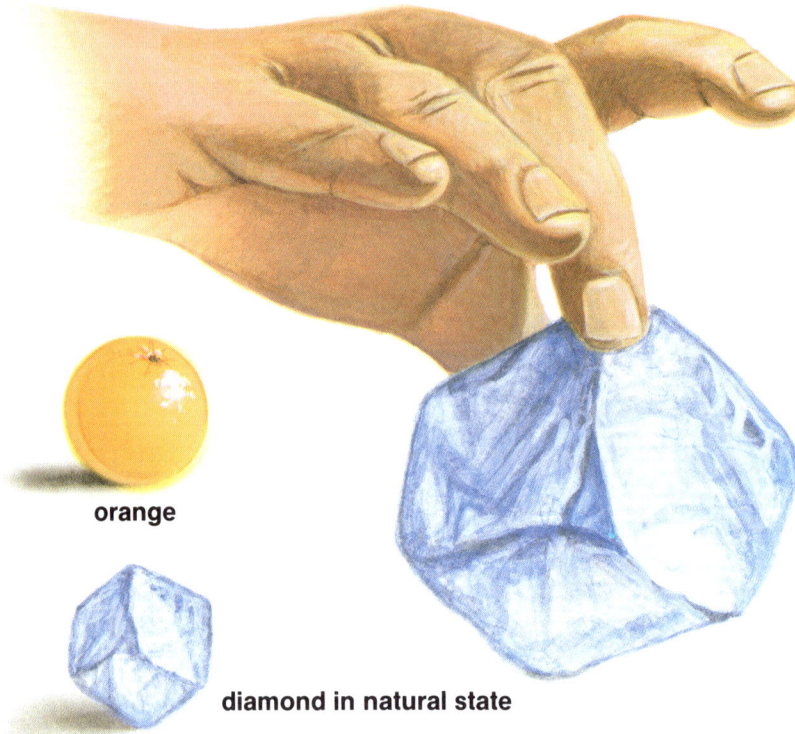

orange

diamond in natural state

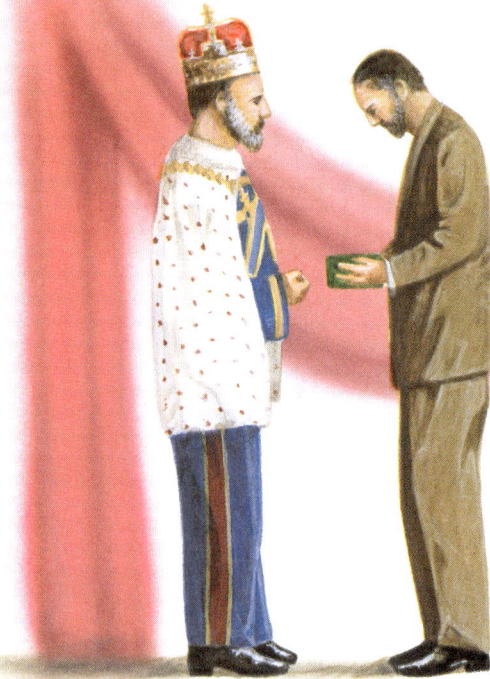

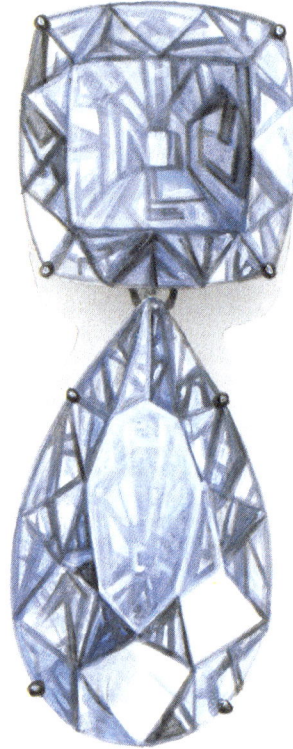

Star of Africa

In 1907 the uncut diamond was sent to King Edward VII of England for his birthday. To fool possible diamond thieves, a guarded empty box was sent to the king. The diamond itself was mailed in a plain box. King Edward chose a Dutch lapidary named Joseph Asscher to cut and polish the diamond. Again, to trick any would-be robbers, an empty box guarded by the British Navy was shipped to Holland, but the valuable diamond was carried in Joseph Asscher's pocket! In Holland, he cut the diamond into nine large gems and ninety-six small ones. The largest became a royal jewel called the Star of Africa.

Opaque Gems

Some gems are opaque rather than transparent—you can't see through them. *Opaque gems* aren't as valuable as transparent ones. They are shaped and polished but not cut. Sometimes opaque **jade** and **carnelian** gemstones are carved. Green is the most common color of jade, but the stone also comes in many other colors.

Some opaque gems have metals that you can see inside them. **Lapis lazuli**, for example, a blue gem, sometimes has flecks of yellow metal called *pyrite*. Because pyrite looks like gold, it is nicknamed "fool's gold."

Gems Made in a Furnace

Gemstones were formed over millions of years in underground rock. They were made by movements that squeezed the rock and brought about changes. Often the rocks got so hot, they melted!

Today, scientists can make some kinds of gems by heating, squeezing, and cooling rocks in furnaces. These are called *synthetic gems,* but you have to look at them under a microscope to tell them apart from gems formed in the earth.

Scientists are successful in making artificial **emeralds**. When found in the earth, these green gems are the softest of the more valuable gemstones. Gem hunters often find them damaged. The **peridot** gem is unusual. It's often called the *evening emerald*. In daylight, it looks yellowish. In lamplight, it looks green!

emerald in natural state

polished emerald

peridot

peridot in daylight

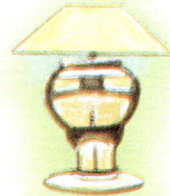

peridot in lamplight

Jewels From Trees

Pines and other evergreen trees have been on earth for millions of years. They contain a sticky substance called *resin*. If the tree bark is injured, resin oozes out and forms a protective lumpy covering over the wound. Insects often get caught and die inside the resin.

In trees that died and rotted long ago, lumps of buried resin hardened into a yellow-brown "gem" called **amber**. Amber can be transparent or opaque. Insect bodies, suspended inside amber, look just as they did when they got trapped there 100 million years ago!

Rainbow Gems

Opal gemstones sparkle with all the colors of the rainbow. They are called *iridescent gems*. The different colors aren't part of the opal itself. They appear because of the way light hits the stone. The colors show up best in round polished opals. These colorful gems are delicate and must be dug by hand, not by machine.

sapphire

ruby

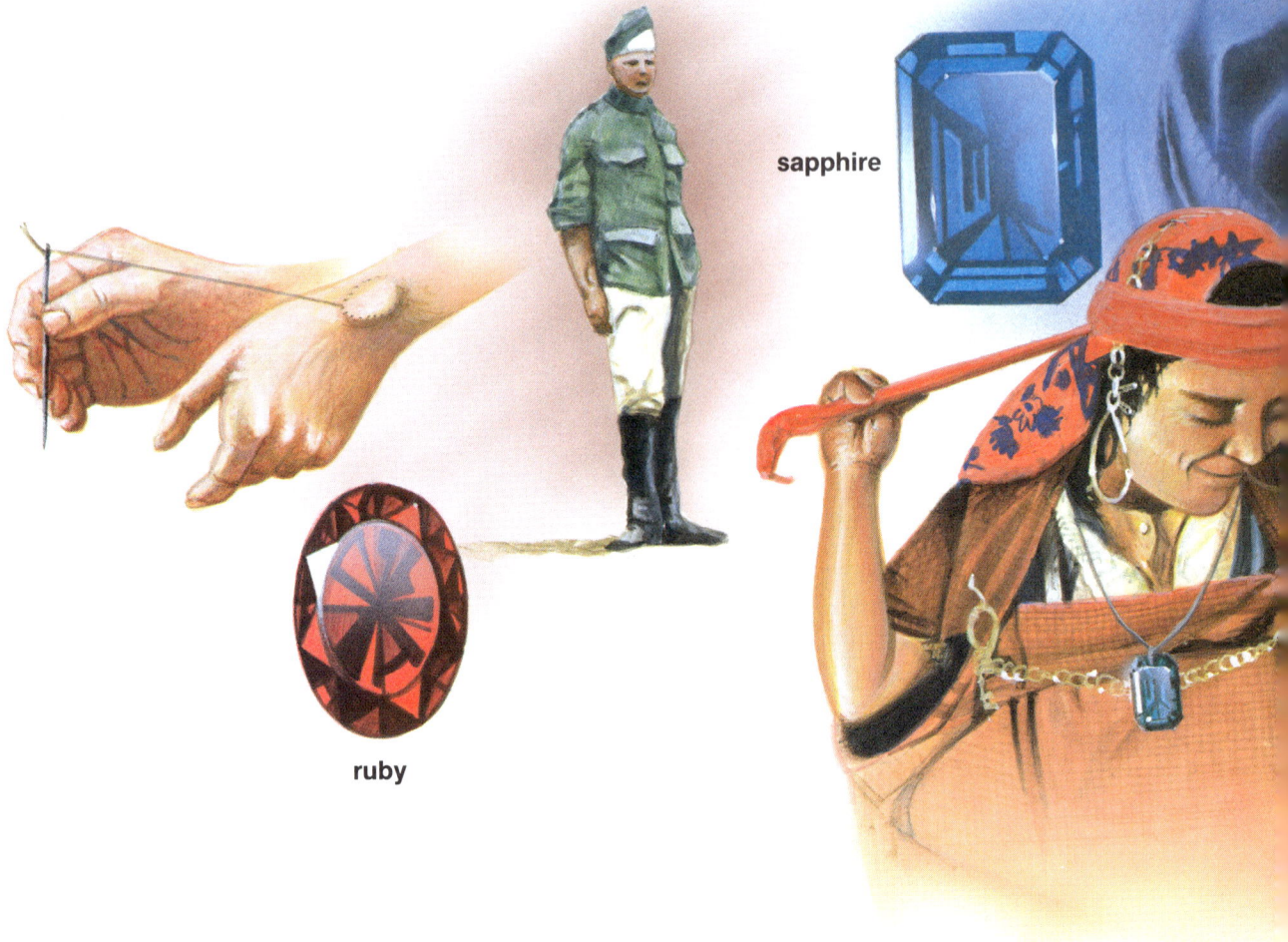

Gemstone Tales

For thousands of years, some people believed that gems had special powers. Soldiers from Burma sewed rubies under their skin to keep them safe in battle. Other people wore sapphires to keep them safe from witches. Sapphires were also thought to be a cure for eye disease. Moonstones were worn to ward off illness. Emeralds were used for digestive problems, and ground-up diamonds were fed to sick people. An amethyst worn on a cord of dog hair was said to cure snakebite!

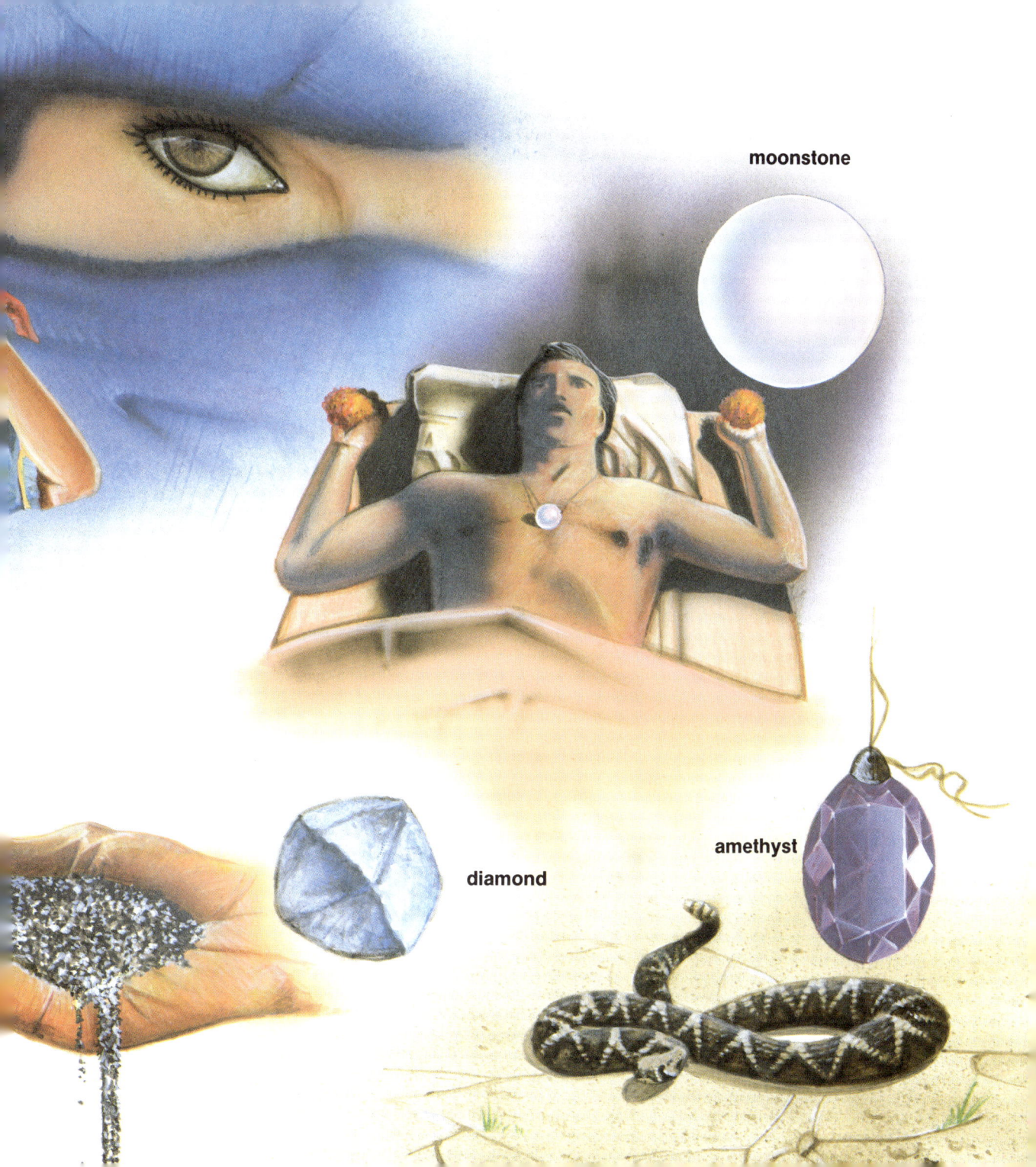

moonstone

diamond

amethyst

Gems of the World

There are hundreds of kinds of gemstones. This map shows where the most popular ones are found.

Gern
Blood

Czechoslovaki
Opal

Austria
Tiger Eye

Jade
Emerald
Turquoise
Opal
Sapphire
Amethyst

Lapis Lazuli
Peridot
Garnet
Rose Quartz
Moonstone

United States

Honduras
Opal

Mexico
Opal
Peridot

Brazil
Diamond
Aquamarine
Emerald
Sapphire
Topaz

Uruguay
Amethyst

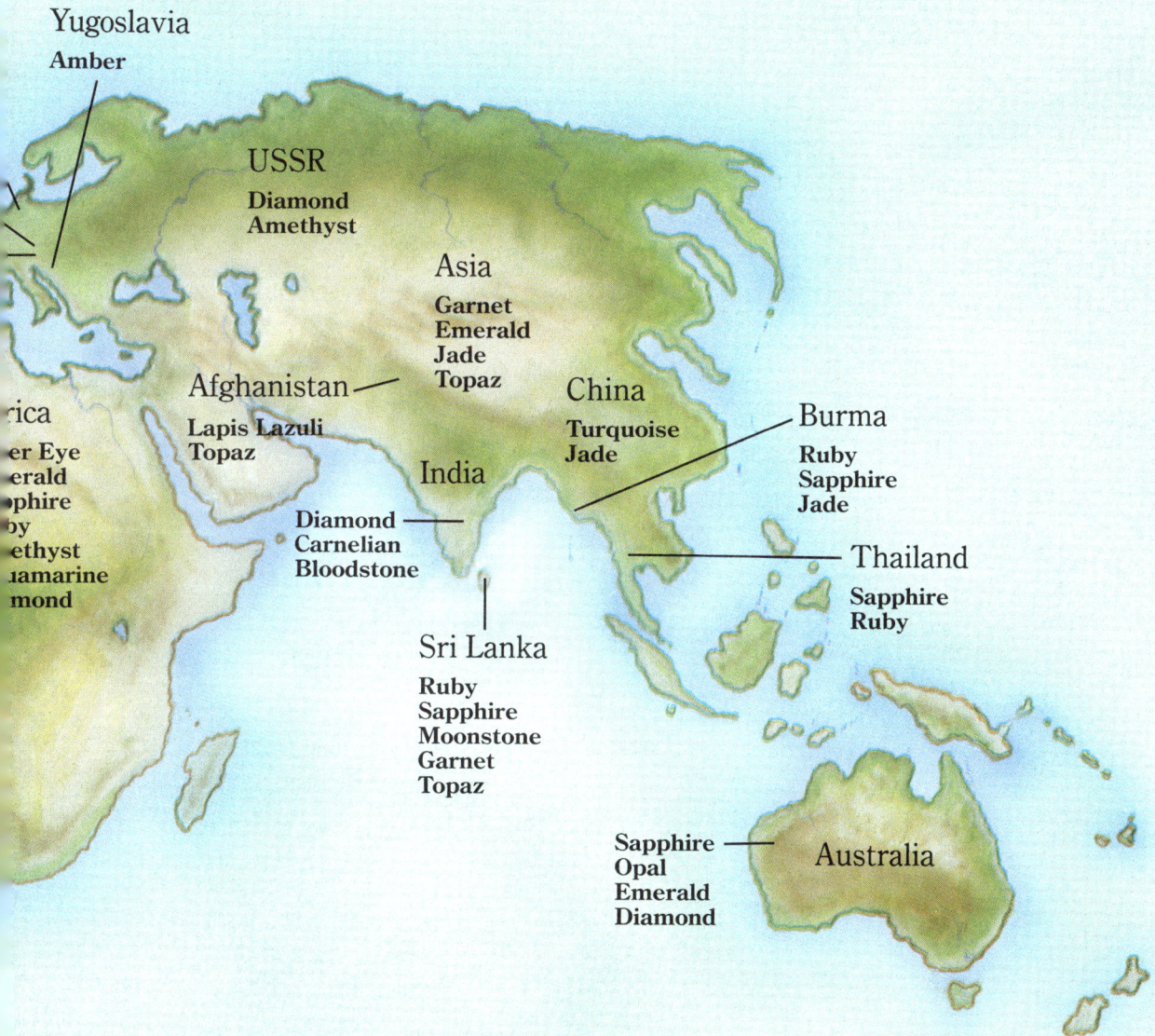

Yugoslavia
Amber

USSR
Diamond
Amethyst

Asia
Garnet
Emerald
Jade
Topaz

Afghanistan
Lapis Lazuli
Topaz

China
Turquoise
Jade

Burma
Ruby
Sapphire
Jade

India
Diamond
Carnelian
Bloodstone

Thailand
Sapphire
Ruby

rica
er Eye
erald
phire
by
ethyst
uamarine
mond

Sri Lanka
Ruby
Sapphire
Moonstone
Garnet
Topaz

Sapphire
Opal
Emerald
Diamond
Australia

January—Garnet

February—Amethyst

March—Aquamarine
or Bloodstone

April—Diamond

May—Emerald

June—Moonstone
or Pearl

July—Ruby

August—Peridot
or Sardonyx

September—Sapphire

October—Opal
or Tourmaline

November—Topaz

December—Lapis Lazu
or Turquoise

What Is Your Birthstone?

In what month were you born? Some people think it's good
luck to wear their birthstones. There is a different gemstone for
each month of the year. No one knows where or when this
custom started, but people have worn birthstone gems for a
long time.